Too Long Unspoken

Jennifer Thorne

ISBN 978-0-578-83476-4

CONTENTS

PART I

CONTENTS

PART II

PART I

UNFORGETTABLE TRUTHS

I pour my heart onto these pages, sharing a glimpse into my trauma and personal heartaches. What I share, was not easy. These moments have left an imprint, impacting me deeply.
These are not good memories, experiences, and feelings that I share, but they are mine. Allowing myself to express these things through poetry has offered me a creative way to work through and process some of which continue to linger, that I have yet to heal.

EMOTIONAL DEPRIVATION

EARLY ON IN LIFE
I HAD BECOME ACCUSTOMED
TO BEING MISTREATED
ON THE REPEATED
IT BECAME NORMAL
NEVER SEEING THE GOOD, ONLY THE BAD
THROUGH LONELY YOUNG EYES
OF A CHILD, ALWAYS SO SAD

ABANDONMENT ISSUES

I'LL NEVER FORGET HOW YOU DIDN'T WANT ME
HOW YOU JUST DUMPED ME
I SUPPOSE YOU WERE JUST
TOO PREOCCUPIED
TOO SELF POSSESSED
YOU NEVER CAME AROUND
SO
I USED TO PLAY PRETEND
BUT EVENTUALLY
AS I GOT OLDER
THE PAIN OF THE TRUTH
AND THE HEARTACHE SET IN
I REALIZED YOU'D NEVER REALLY LOVE ME
FINALLY I ALLOWED MYSELF TO TAKE THAT IN
BUT
NO MATTER THE AMOUNT OF ACCEPTANCE
IT SEEMS AS THOUGH
THIS DEEP SADNESS
AND LONGING
WILL NEVER TRULY END

INNOCENCE STOLEN

I WAS JUST A CHILD
WHEN MY INNOCENCE WAS STOLEN
NO MORE SEEING THE WORLD
THROUGH A LENS COLORED GOLDEN
NO MORE MYSTERY
NO MORE MAGIC
EVERYTHING SEEMED DELUDED
IT WAS TRAGIC
ONLY VIOLENCE
DISGUST
AND SHAME REMAINED
I WOULD NEVER BE THE SAME

ASSAULT

Woke up in a haze
Pants unbuttoned
pushed way down below my waist
Trying to make it to the bathroom
so much pain
blood trickling
flesh ripped
Flashes of blurred memory surface
Trying to get a grip
calm down
"How did I deserve this?"

UNSUSPECTED PREDATOR

Is it only me, who truly sees you
Your distorted thoughts
horrible intentions
The depths of your eyes, tell truth
Where the soul should set, something else stirs
It wanted nothing more than to play a charade
To get close, and cut deep
causing only discontentment and pain
It is all consuming
no second thought need be
No empathy, nor moral compass
And in its wake
left nothing more of me

IMPRISONED

I FIND MYSELF CONFINED
HELD CAPTIVE WITHIN MY OWN DARKNESS
HAUNTED BY THE INESCAPABLE MISFORTUNES OF THE PAST
WITH DEEP SCARS AND FEELINGS OF INADEQUACY
NOT KNOWING HOW TO BREAK THE CYCLE
I CONTINUE TO WALK BESIDE WHAT IS FAMILIAR
WILL THIS EVER END?

THE NARCISSIST

He was beautiful, charming
Everything she could ever dream
Then things began to unravel
leaving her broken, empty
He was nothing as he had seemed
The mask came off
with truth revealed
Nothing was left for him to conceal
And
with him, pieces of her went
Pieces she longed for
searched for
Hoping it was time well spent

FICTIONAL CHARACTER

Although your love was a fallacy
a farce
I'd be lying if I said it hasn't been hard
Letting go the fictional character you played quite well
The Façade
put me under your spell
I find myself yearning for someone
who's not even real
The mask
who captured my heart for the steal
Because you were the first
to give me more than just some possessive glance
You gave kindness
and warmth
that I've never known
I became addicted to the way you loved me

THE CYCLE CONTINUES

You said you'd never hurt me
yet your hands are wrapped around my throat
I hit the wall
falling to the ground
seemingly
too weak to crawl
I sit
contemplating why
I always allow myself
to end up in these same situations

You said you were different
yet all you do is take
Devouring what little has been left of me
And
at this point
after it all
I'm too brittle to bend
so I break

CONSUMED

They say you'll "get over it"
but I find it dictates every part of my life
I trust no one
I attract the wrong type
I can't quite grasp love, to save my life
My resentment grows for the opposite sex
Here I am though, despite it all
trying to love myself
trying to do what I think is best

RAGE

AFTER AWHILE
YOU BECOME ADDICTED TO THE RAGE
IT'S THE ONLY THING LEFT
THAT MAKES YOU FEEL SANE
WHEN EVERYTHING ELSE IS BROKEN
STOLEN
SOMETIMES I FIND MYSELF
TOO FAR GONE
AND SO OUTSPOKEN

PART II

PLACING FLOWERS

My placing of flowers
in the absence of things long lost.

"

BEAUTY CAN ARISE FROM THE DEEPEST, DARKEST OF PLACES

WHAT THE CHAOS LEFT

SIFTING THROUGH WHAT THE CHAOS LEFT
FINDING THE PIECES
UTILIZING THE BEST
BEAUTY CAN ARISE FROM THE DEEPEST, DARKEST OF PLACES
REMEMBER THAT NEXT TIME YOU FEEL FIXATED
FRUSTRATED
UNHEARD
AND
UNSEEN
ON ALL THINGS DONE TO YOU THAT CAN NOT BE REDEEMED
I UNDERSTAND THE RAGE
THE PAIN
THE TORMENT YOU FEEL
BUT WE MUST LET GO OF IT
IT'S POISON
IT WILL DO NOTHING TO HELP YOU HEAL

SELF SABOTAGE

Stop over compensating, for what you've endured and lost
Debauchery in its self, isn't worth the cost
I know it's hard when
you've been tossed around
snuffed out, and internally lost
but
escapism
isolation, and self medication
will only numb things for awhile
Eventually
you'll begin to overindulge
creating a viscous cycle
After so long
you have to
release yourself from the grips of denial
These decisions
this emotional self sabotage
self deprecation
will only do more damage
Not allowing you, to fully heal and to grow
Trust me, I've been there
I know

LEAVE IT LIE

WHY LIST THE WAYS YOU TORMENT ME
HAVEN'T I ENDURED ENOUGH
WITH SOAKED EYES, HALLOWED CHEEKS
AND TATTERED VISIONS OF YOU
I SEEK REFUGE IN THE SAFETY OF MY OWN WARMTH
I LIGHT MY OWN CANDLE
I SHOW MYSELF THE WAY

FORGIVENESS

Forgiveness isn't about acceptance
saying that what happened was ok
It's about moving on
releasing
and peering inward
way down deep
so that you may
Use that pain for mending yourself
as well as others
who also may need
your unique insights
and strengths

DARE TO LOVE

Brave hearts
Those who dare love
after such immeasurable pain
It is you
your fearlessness
that sparks hope
Lighting the way through the depths
of internal darkness
Guiding truth in the vastness
of others suffering

SELF EXPANSION

THE DARKER SIDE WHICH GRIPS YOU TIGHT
ISN'T A CURSE
BUT A WAY INTO THE LIGHT

YOUR DEMONS CAN BECOME YOUR SAVIORS
IF YOU SO CHOOSE

THROUGH HEALTHY EXPRESSION
OF YOUR OWN INTERNALIZED PAIN
SELF EXPANSION CAN BE OBTAINED

www.ingramcontent.com/pod-product-compliance
Lightning Source LLC
Chambersburg PA
CBHW020449030426
42337CB00014B/1471